Horses, Donkeys, and Mules in the MARINES

AMERICA'S Animal Soldiers

by Meish Goldish

Consultant: Anthony Parkhurst
Training Specialist
Pack-Master, Marine Corps Mountain Warfare Training Center

BEARPORT
PUBLISHING

New York, New York

Credits

Cover and Title Page, © U.S. Marine Corps/Cpl. Nichole A. LaVine and Science Faction/SuperStock; 4, © AP Photo; 5, Courtesy of Nancy Latham Parkin Collection; 6, © Robert Nickelsberg/Getty Images; 7, © U.S. Marine Corps Photo/Sgt. Ben J. Flores; 8L, © U.S. Marine Corps Photo/Cpl. Andrew S. Avitt; 8R, © U.S. Marine Corps Photo/Mountain Warfare Training Center; 9, Copyright © 2011, Los Angeles Times/Don Bartletti; 10, © Image Asset Management/World History Archive/AGE Fotostock; 11, © Robert Nickelsberg/Getty Images; 12, Copyright © 2011, Los Angeles Times/Don Bartletti; 13, Copyright © 2011, Los Angeles Times/ Don Bartletti; 14, Copyright © 2011, Los Angeles Times/Don Bartletti; 15, © U.S. Marine Corps Photo/CPL K.B. Manago; 16, Copyright © 2011, Los Angeles Times/Don Bartletti; 17, Copyright © 2011, Los Angeles Times/Don Bartletti; 18TL, © Robert Preston Photography/Alamy; 18TR, © John Warburton-Lee Photography/Alamy; 18B, © Michael Zegers Collection/imagebroker/ AGE Fotostock; 19, © Science Faction/SuperStock; 20, © Science Faction/SuperStock; 21, © U.S. Marine Corps Photo/LCPL Stephen Kwietniak; 22TL, © Kay Nietfeld/dpa/Landov; 22TR, © AP Photo/Kingman Daily Miner/JC Amberlyn; 22BL, © Bart Ah You/ZUMA Press/Corbis; 22BR, © Danilo Donadoni/Marka/AGE Fotostock.

Publisher: Kenn Goin
Editorial Director: Adam Siegel
Creative Director: Spencer Brinker
Design: Debrah Kaiser
Photo Researcher: Picture Perfect Professionals, LLC

Library of Congress Cataloging-in-Publication Data

Goldish, Meish.
  Horses, donkeys, and mules in the Marines / by Meish Goldish ; consultant, Anthony Parkhurst.
       p. cm. — (America's animal soldiers)
  Includes bibliographical references and index.
  Audience: Ages 7-12.
  ISBN-13: 978-1-61772-453-4 (library binding)
  ISBN-10: 1-61772-453-X (library binding)
  1. War horses—United States—Juvenile literature. 2. Mules—War use—United States—Juvenile literature. 3. Pack animals (Transportation)—United States—Juvenile literature. 4. United States. Marine Corps—Juvenile literature. I. Parkhurst, Anthony. II. Title.
  UC603.G65 2012
  359.9'6—dc23
                                2011034728

For more information, write to Bearport Publishing Company, Inc., 45 West 21st Street, Suite 3B, New York, New York 10010. Printed in the United States of America in North Mankato, Minnesota.

10 9 8 7 6 5 4 3 2 1

CONTENTS

Reckless to the Rescue

In the early 1950s, U.S. **Marines** were risking their lives fighting in the **Korean War.** To fire at enemy tanks, they used a powerful weapon called the **recoilless rifle.** It weighed so much that it took three or four men to carry it. The **shells** it fired were also heavy. Each one weighed 24 pounds (11 kg)—as much as two bowling balls. A Marine could carry only three or four rifle shells at a time. As a result, the Marines needed a faster way to bring the **ammunition** to the **front lines**. Luckily, they found Reckless.

Soldiers in Korea using a recoilless rifle

Reckless was a female racehorse that the Marines bought while they were fighting in Korea. They trained her to carry up to ten shells on her back. During one battle, Reckless delivered nearly 10,000 pounds (4,536 kg) of ammunition over five days. The courageous horse was able to make 51 trips to the front lines in one day. Despite enemy fire, Reckless bravely carried out her job, even bringing wounded Marines back to the **base camp**.

Reckless was made a **sergeant** in the Marines for her bravery. She received the **Purple Heart** twice, plus other awards, for her heroic acts.

Reckless carrying a load of shells

Animal Advantages

Reckless isn't the only horse that has served in the U.S. **military**. During wartime, Marines have used many horses, as well as **donkeys** and **mules**, to carry their weapons and supplies. By carrying these heavy loads, the **pack animals** help Marines stay safe. Without the extra weight on their backs, Marines can move around more quickly.

This mule carries a heavy load for Marines.

Pack animals can carry much more weight on their backs than people can. For example, a mule can carry about 300 pounds (136 kg) and a donkey can carry around 125 pounds (57 kg). A Marine, however, can carry only about 75 to 100 pounds (34 to 45 kg).

Pack animals offer other advantages, too. They can move across ground where supply trucks cannot pass. For example, Marines have been fighting in the mountains of Afghanistan since the early 2000s. There are no roads for **vehicles** in parts of the country. Yet horses, donkeys, and mules can easily cross the rough and rocky **terrain**.

Arctic Ocean

ASIA

NORTH AMERICA

EUROPE

Atlantic Ocean

AFRICA

Pacific Ocean

Pacific Ocean

SOUTH AMERICA

Indian Ocean

AUSTRALIA

N W E S

Southern Ocean

ANTARCTICA

Afghanistan is located in southwestern Asia.

Pack animals travel easily on rocky ground where there are no roads.

A Place to Train

Most Marines have no experience working with horses, donkeys, or mules before they join the military. To learn about these pack animals—and how to use them in the mountains—they take a two-week training course. It's held at the Marine Corps Mountain Warfare Training Center in California's Sierra Nevada mountains. At the training center, some mountains rise more than two miles (3.2 km) high. With few roads around, **trainees** quickly discover the advantages of using animals to carry their supplies.

The Marine Corps Mountain Warfare Training Center is located in California on 46,000 acres (18,616 hectares) of the Humboldt-Toiyabe National Forest.

The Mountain Warfare Training Center opened in 1951 to teach American troops how to fight in mountains during the Korean War.

Why don't Marines simply use helicopters instead of animals to carry their supplies? Helicopters can be easy to spot. As a result, they may give away the location of troops to the enemy. Pack animals, however, are not as easy to see. They can bring supplies to an area without the enemy ever finding out.

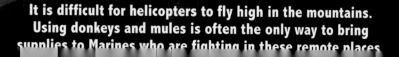

It is difficult for helicopters to fly high in the mountains. Using donkeys and mules is often the only way to bring supplies to Marines who are fighting in these remote places.

History Class

During their first day at the Mountain Warfare Training Center, Marines get a history lesson. **Instructors** speak about battles that were won with the help of pack animals. They talk about a famous Marine hero, Sergeant Major Daniel Daly. He earned a **Medal of Honor** for leading pack animals into battle in Haiti in 1915.

About 2,200 years ago, the famous general Hannibal used pack animals to carry weapons and supplies when his army crossed the **Alps** to fight the Romans in Italy. He also brought a few elephants to break through enemy lines.

This painting shows Hannibal's army struggling to cross the Alps.

Marines also learn the history of the training course. It began in the 1980s, after the Soviet Union **invaded** Afghanistan. The United States opposed the Soviets' **occupation** of the country, so the U.S. **Central Intelligence Agency** (CIA) sent several thousand mules to Afghanistan. The animals made it easier for the Afghan army to move its weapons and supplies through the mountains. Because the CIA also needed to send people who could work with the mules, the training course was set up at that time as well.

In addition to mules, Afghan soldiers used horses to carry food and supplies.

Packing It On

A single pack animal can carry a lot of equipment. Marines learn to load machine guns, **mortars**, **grenades**, missiles, and rifle ammunition onto their animals. They also add food, water, blankets, sleeping bags, boots, helmets, and medical supplies.

Marines learn how to pack large loads onto their animals.

Besides learning how to pack equipment, Marines learn to use their animals to carry injured and dead soldiers. Trainees practice with 180-pound (82-kg) **dummies** called Rescue Randys.

A heavy load is no problem for horses, donkeys, and mules. However, trainees must be able to balance the items on their animals so the load doesn't sag to one side. Marines practice packing and unpacking their equipment over and over again. They even learn to pack their animals in the dark.

A Marine practices strapping supplies onto a mule so that the animal feels comfortable.

Learning the Ropes

A pack animal can easily bear the weight of a heavy load. However, the equipment must be tied **securely** with rope. Otherwise, the load will shift and possibly damage the equipment or injure the animal. During their training, Marines get hands-on experience working with rope. They practice using it not only to secure supplies, but also to lead the pack animals in the right direction.

A Marine learning how to lead his donkey

Marines also learn how to tie many different kinds of knots in rope. Each knot serves a specific purpose. Instructors, like Sergeant Graham Golden, stress the importance of handling the ropes correctly. "Pull that rope tight," he tells the Marines. "You're not going to hurt the mule, and otherwise that load is going to fall off up the mountain."

As part of their training, Marines practice tying knots while blindfolded.

After trainees spend several days tying knots hundreds of times, they are graded on their skill.

In the Mood

While at the training center, Marines learn to do something even more important than packing and tying loads on their animals' backs. They learn how to feed and care for their four-legged friends. "You have to keep them healthy, or knowing how to strap a pack on them won't mean anything," said Lance Corporal Timothy L. Huff.

Marines learn how to feed their animals to keep them healthy and strong.

The pack animals used at the training center do not travel overseas with the Marines. Instead, the Marines get other horses, donkeys, and mules in the places where they are sent to fight.

As Marines take care of their animals, they get to know each one's particular behavior. "They all have their own **quirks** and personalities," said Sergeant Joe Neal, an instructor. There is one trait, however, that most donkeys share. They do not respond well to rough treatment or harsh language. When two Marines tried to pull and push their donkey up a steep trail, the animal stopped moving. It snorted and **brayed** loudly. The trainees eventually learned that being gentle and offering food work much better than being rough.

Marines need to learn how to deal with a stubborn donkey.

The Same but Different

By the end of their training, Marines know all about pack animals. They understand how the different creatures are similar. For example, horses, donkeys, and mules can all handle heavy loads. All three pack animals can also walk on steep, rocky ground. However, the Marines learn that there are important differences, too.

horses

mule

donkey

Most packhorses weigh about 1,200 to 1,500 pounds (544 to 680 kg). A mule usually weighs about 1,000 pounds (454 kg) and a donkey weighs about 500 pounds (227 kg).

For example, mules are more **cautious** than horses. A horse would run off a cliff if it was instructed to do so. Mules would not, because they have a stronger sense of **survival**. They often refuse to move forward because they sense the path they're being asked to travel is too dangerous.

A mule can carry a heavy load 7 hours a day for 20 days straight without complaining.

A horse or donkey can carry a load equal to 25 percent of its body weight. A mule can carry up to 33 percent of its body weight.

The Future for Marine Pack Animals

Will horses, donkeys, and mules continue to serve the Marines in the future? That depends on where America's future wars will be fought. For more than 100 years, pack animals were used in U.S. wars. By the 1950s, however, most of them had been replaced by trucks and other vehicles, which could deliver weapons and supplies faster than animals.

Motor vehicles, such as this Humvee, are useful only when there are paths they can travel on.

Today, however, America finds itself battling enemies in places like the mountains of Afghanistan. The lack of roads puts pack animals in demand again. Despite modern vehicles, it is likely that horses, donkeys, and mules will continue to serve Marines faithfully in the years ahead.

There are about 5 donkeys, 29 mules, and 11 horses at the Marine Corps Mountain Warfare Training Center.

More About
Horses, Donkeys, and Mules

Horses, donkeys, and mules serve the U.S. Marines. However, these animals also help people in many other ways. Here are some examples.

Police horses help officers move quickly in places where there are many people, as well as keep the crowds under control.

Therapy horses help people with physical disabilities strengthen their muscles and improve their balance.

Mules help farmers grow their crops by pulling plows in a field.

Donkeys carry people who travel up or down mountains or canyons.

Glossary

Alps (ALPS) a large group of mountains in Europe that stretches for about 660 miles (1,062 km) through parts of Austria, Italy, Switzerland, Germany, France, Slovenia, and Liechtenstein

ammunition (*am*-yuh-NISH-uhn) objects that are fired from weapons, such as bullets

base camp (BAYSS KAMP) a safe center for military operations; often a place where soldiers live and from which they operate

brayed (BRAYD) made a loud, unpleasant noise

cautious (KAW-shuhss) careful and watchful

Central Intelligence Agency (SEN-truhl in-TEL-uh-juhns AY-juhn-see) an American organization that gathers information in foreign countries for the U.S. government

donkeys (DONG-keez) long-eared animals that are related to horses but are smaller

dummies (DUHM-eez) objects made to represent human bodies

front lines (FRUHNT LYENZ) areas where battles take place in wars

grenades (gruh-NAYDZ) small bombs that are thrown by hand

instructors (in-STRUHK-turz) teachers

invaded (in-VAYD-id) entered by force or took over, usually in a harmful way

Korean War (kuh-REE-uhn WOR) a war that was fought from 1950 to 1953 between North Korea and South Korea; U.S. soldiers fought on the side of South Korea

Marines (muh-REENZ) a branch of the U.S. military; Marines are trained to fight on both land and at sea

Medal of Honor (MED-uhl UHV ON-ur) the highest military award given by the U.S. government

military (MIL-uh-*ter*-ee) the armed forces of a country

mortars (MOR-turz) very short cannons that fire explosives high in the air

mules (MYOOLZ) animals produced by mating a female horse (called a mare) with a male donkey (called a jack)

occupation (ok-yuh-PAY-shuhn) when a country takes control of another country

pack animals (PAK AN-uh-muhlz) animals used to carry heavy loads

Purple Heart (PUR-puhl HART) a U.S. military award given by the president to those who have been wounded or killed while serving in the U.S. military

quirks (KWURKS) strange ways of acting

recoilless rifle (ri-KOIL-uhss RYE-fuhl) a type of long, heavy weapon used to fire shells at tanks

securely (si-KYOOR-lee) tightly and firmly

sergeant (SAR-juhnt) a noncommissioned officer in the Marine Corps who is in charge of troops

shells (SHELZ) hollow metal cases filled with explosives that are fired from a rifle or another kind of gun

survival (sur-VYE-vuhl) the act of staying alive

terrain (tuh-RAYN) ground or land

trainees (tray-NEEZ) people who are learning a particular skill

vehicles (VEE-uh-kuhlz) machines, such as cars and trucks, that carry people or goods from one place to another

Index

Bibliography

Hodges, Meredith. *Training Mules and Donkeys: A Logical Approach to Longears*. Loveland, CO: Lucky Three Productions (2003).

Kistler, John M. *Animals in the Military: From Hannibal's Elephants to the Dolphins of the U.S. Navy*. Santa Barbara, CA: ABC-CLIO (2011).

Orlean, Susan. "Riding High: Mules in the Military." *The New Yorker* (February 15, 2010).

Perry, Tony. "Marines' Beasts of Burden Are Again Leading the Pack." *Los Angeles Times* (July 7, 2009).

Read More

Goldish, Meish. *Marine Corps: Civilian to Marine (Becoming a Soldier)*. New York: Bearport (2011).

Grayson, Robert. *Military (Working Animals)*. Tarrytown, NY: Marshall Cavendish Benchmark (2011).

Grayson, Robert. *Transportation (Working Animals)*. Tarrytown, NY: Marshall Cavendish Benchmark (2011).

Murray, Julie. *Military Animals (Going to Work)*. Edina, MN: ABDO (2009).

Sandler, Michael. *Military Horses (Horse Power)*. New York: Bearport (2007).

Learn More Online

To learn more about horses, donkeys, and mules in the U.S. Marines, visit
www.bearportpublishing.com/AmericasAnimalSoldiers

About the Author

Meish Goldish has written more than 200 books for children. He lives in Brooklyn, New York.